# MELVIL ᴀɴᴅ DEWEY
# TEACH LITERACY

# MELVIL AND DEWEY TEACH LITERACY

## A Teaching Guide to Using the Melvil and Dewey Series

*Pamela Curtis Swallow*

*Illustrated by Lorena Eliasen*

A Member of the Greenwood Publishing Group

Westport, Connecticut • London

*For librarians, teachers and students
everywhere.*

British Library Cataloguing in Publication Data is available.

Text copyright (c) 2004 by Pamela Swallow Curtis
Illustrations copyright (c) 2004 by Lorena Eliasen

ISBN: 1-59158-179-6 (set)
      1-59158-150-8 (Melvil and Dewey in the Chips)
      1-59158-151-6 (Melvil and Dewey in the Fast Lane)
      1-59158-153-2 (Melvil and Dewey Gone Fishin')
      1-59158-152-4 (Melvil and Dewey Teach Literacy)

First published in 2004

Libraries Unlimited, 88 Post Road West, Westport, CT 06881
A Member of the Greenwood Publishing Group, Inc.
www.lu.com

Printed in the United States of America

The paper used in this book complies with the
Permanent Paper Standard issued by the National
Information Standards Organization (Z39.48–1984).

10   9   8   7   6   5   4   3   2   1

# CONTENTS

# MELVIL AND DEWEY
## TEACH LITERACY
### (NEVER UNDERESTIMATE THE POWER OF SMALL RODENTS)

This activity guide has been created by Melvil, Dewey, Pam, and Lorena, to be fun, as well as instructional. You'll find varied groups of lively activities, designed to connect students with ideas, learning skills and information.

We said "fun," but don't worry—we've taken into account Howard Gardner's theory of multiple intelligences, Bloom's Taxonomy of cognitive processes, and the American Association of School Librarian's Nine Information Literacy Standards for Student Learning. So you're all set.

The activities may be done by individual students, teams, or an entire class. With the exception of the taxonomy levels and literacy standards listed at the end of each activity, the wording of the activities is directed toward pupils rather than adult facilitators. With the selections offered in each of the categories, the options are plentiful. It's a smorgasbord. Dig in!

# DOING DEWEY PROUD
## (LIBRARY SKILLS)

### Melvil Dewey Who?

Our favorite gerbils were named after a famous man, Melvil Dewey. Who was he, and what did he do? Find information about this "Father of Librarianship." Can you find out what his whole name was? It was a long time ago that he became famous. You are living in a more modern age. If you were given the task of organizing libraries, how would you do it? Design a library that you would really enjoy.

- *Bloom's Taxonomy Level 1 (knowledge), Level 3 (application), and Level 5 (synthesis)*

- *Information Literacy Standard 1 (accessing information) and Standard 3 (using information)*

### What's Mr. Dewey's System All About?

Melvil Dewey liked things to be organized. He also liked mathematics. When he was a young man, he was bothered by the fact that no two libraries arranged their books in the same way. So he fixed that. He invented a system that groups books into subject areas. He gave each subject a number. Look at the books in your library's non-fiction area. You will see Melvil Dewey's "Dewey Decimal Numbers" on the spines. The numbers are like addresses, showing where the books belong on the shelf.

Notice that many of these books contain facts about particular subjects. But also notice that not all nonfiction books are "true." Their subjects may be fairytales, myths, plays, or the "unknown," but they each have a number that keeps the books grouped together by topic. Very handy.

*Here are two activities to help you understand how the Dewey Decimal System works.*

**Activity One.** The Dewey Decimal System starts with ten general classes of knowledge. Within these large categories, there are smaller ones, each representing a certain subject.

Divide your class into teams of two or three students. Have each team take a section of the nonfiction collection to examine, using Melvil Dewey's 10 major classes: 000–099, 100–199, 200–299, 300–399, 400–499, 500–599, 600–699, 700–799, 800–899, 900–999. After the teams have examined their sections for about ten minutes, have them report back to the class about what they learned and noticed. Teams can then make shelf signs for their sections.

**Activity Two.** After you have learned about the different subject areas in the nonfiction section, bring in some of your toys and assign each one its correct Dewey Decimal number. For example, a panda would be given the number 599.74, a toy dinosaur would get the number 567.9, and a puzzle would be 793.73, and so on. You will soon see how Melvil Dewey's system works. Arrange your toys around the room in Dewey order. You have created a toy library!

- *Bloom's Taxonomy Level 2 (comprehension) and Level 3 (application)*

- *Information Literacy Standard 2 (evaluating information) and Standard 3 (using information)*

## Extra! Extra! Read All about 'Em!

Gerbils are *very* interesting—just ask Melvil and Dewey. Find out more about these lovable animals. Look in lots of different places to gather your information (nature books, encyclopedias, Internet sites, videos, magazines, etc.). Here's a worksheet to help you out.

1. Where do gerbils live in the wild? Describe their environment.

   _____

   _____

2. What is their life in the wild like?

   _____

   _____

3. What sort of homes do they make? Describe or draw a gerbil burrow.

   _____

   _____

4. What do they eat? Where do they get this food?

   _____

   _____

5. What is gerbil behavior like? What are their habits?

   _____

   _____

6. How often do gerbils reproduce? Describe baby gerbils and how they develop.

   _____

   _____

* Bonus question: how do gerbils greet each other?

   _____

   _____

- *Bloom's Taxonomy Level 1 (knowledge)*

- *Information Literacy Standard 1 (accessing information)*

# Gerbil Comfort

Pets should be well taken care of. Learn about taking care of pet gerbils—gather your information from lots of different places (pet-care books, magazines, pamphlets, interviews with gerbil owners, pet shops, Web sites, etc.).

What are some of the things you could do to make a pet gerbil comfortable and happy?

`When you are finished gathering your information, ask your teacher or librarian to turn to the back of the activity book and help you compare what you have learned with the advice given by twelve-year-old Ryan Smith, who raises gerbils.

- *Bloom's Taxonomy Level 1 (knowledge) and Level 3 (application)*

- *Information Literacy Standard 1 (accessing information)*

## Click Your Mouse

Dewey is very interested in computers. He'd be proud to know that you can use a computer to learn more about gerbils and other rodents. With the help of Internet reference sites for kids such as Ask Jeeves kids, Lycos Zone, KidsClick! or Yahooligans, find five new facts about the rodent of your choice.

- *Bloom's Taxonomy Level 1 (knowledge)*

- *Information Literacy Standard 1 (accessing information)*

## Predators Have to Eat, Too

Some animals prey on rodents. Melvil and Dewey learned that firsthand! Find out about three kinds of animals that like rodents as meals. Compare and contrast how these predators live and how they eat. Draw a Venn diagram or use Kidspiration software to report your comparison to the class.

- *Bloom's Taxonomy Level 1 (knowledge), Level 2 (comprehension), and Level 4 (analysis)*

- *Information Literacy Standard 1 (accessing information) and Standard 3 (using information accurately and creatively)*

## Pick a Pet

Think of a pet, and then find both a nonfiction book and a fiction book about this animal.

What facts does the author include in the fiction book?

Is there anything in the fiction book that isn't accurate?

What new information did you learn from the nonfiction book?

Write your own short story about this animal.

- *Bloom's Taxonomy Level 1 (knowledge), Level 2 (comprehension), and Level 5 (synthesis)*

- *Information Literacy Standard 1 (accessing information), Standard 2 (evaluating information), and Standard 3 (using information accurately and creatively)*

# Where in the World Is . . . ?

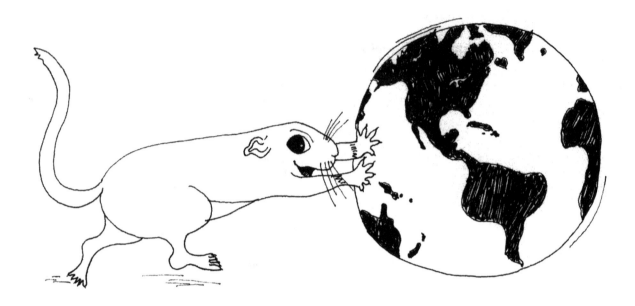

Use an atlas, an encyclopedia, a geographical diction- ary, or an Internet site to locate Maine, where Melvil and Dewey go on vacation with Mrs. Alden. How far from your state is Maine? How many states would you have to drive through to get to Maine?

Bonus! Can you locate Porter Lake?

- *Bloom's Taxonomy Level 1 (knowledge) and Level 2 (comprehension)*

- *Information Literacy Standard 1 (accessing information)*

## Ol' Pete the Pickerel of Porter Lake

Ol' Pete was quite a fish! Research the pickerel. What other fish might be found in a Maine lake? Learn about different kinds of freshwater and saltwater fish and where they can be found. Are there some fish that live in both fresh water and salt water? What are they?

- *Bloom's Taxonomy Level 1 (knowledge) and Level 2 (comprehension)*

- *Information Literacy Standard 1 (accessing information)*

# GRAPH IT, CHART IT, MAP IT!
## (GET VISUAL)

### Rodent Relatives

Gerbils are in the family of animals called rodents. How do they measure up to their rodent cousins?

According to Melvil and Dewey, gerbils are the cutest rodents. But which ones are the biggest? The smallest?

Make a chart comparing and contrasting gerbils with other rodents. Don't forget the two that you meet in *Melvil and Dewey Gone Fishin'*. Do you think a beaver would make a good pet? How about a chipmunk?

- *Bloom's Taxonomy Level 1 (knowledge), Level 2 (comprehension), and Level 4 (analysis)*

- *Information Literacy Standard 2 (evaluating information)*

### Suppose . . .

First, dig for information about how often gerbils are able to have babies. Then, suppose that you have a male and female gerbil and they reproduce, and then *their* babies grow and reproduce, and so on . . . .

Make a chart or diagram showing how fast a gerbil population could grow.

What conclusions can you draw from this?

What if gerbils are released in an environment where they do not normally live? What could happen if they quickly multiply?

- *Bloom's Taxonomy Level 1 (knowledge), Level 4 (analysis), and Level 6 (evaluation)*

- *Information Literacy Standard 1 (accessing information) and Standard 2 (evaluating information)*

# Hey Ho! Hey Ho! Vacation We Will Go!

If you could take the gerbils with you on vacation, where would you go?
What activities could the gerbils do there?
Discuss with your friends the pros and cons of different vacation trips, and then make a graph or chart showing your trip ideas.

- *Bloom's Taxonomy Level 3 (application) and Level 4 (analysis)*

- *Information Literacy Standard 2 (evaluating information)*

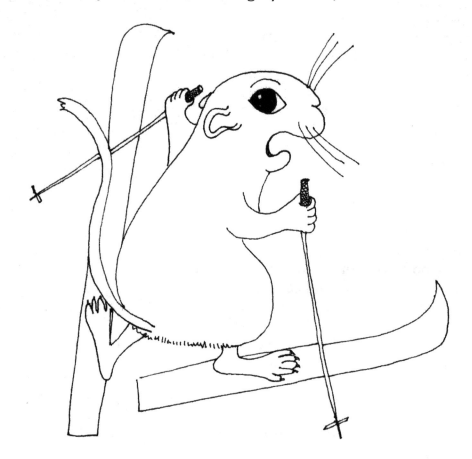

# The Survey Says . . .

Take a survey of students in a classroom, or in your entire school, about the pets they have, or would like to have. Make a graph of popular pets. How do gerbils rate in the survey?

- *Bloom's Taxonomy Level 4 (analysis), Level 5 (synthesis), and Level 6 (evaluation)*

- *Information Literacy Standard 2 (evaluating information)*

# Make a Map

In *Melvil and Dewey in the Fast Lane*, Melvil and Dewey manage to escape from a student's house and return to their school. What if Melvil and Dewey had to get back to school from your house? Draw a map showing the route that they would take.

• *Bloom's Taxonomy Level 3 (application)*

• *Information Literacy Standard 3 (using information accurately and creatively)*

# WRITE ON!
# (CREATIVE WRITING)

## Gerbil Journaling

Keep a diary for several days as Dewey and then as Melvil. How different are their thoughts and feelings about the things that happen to them? How do their personality traits affect your writing? What is it like to be "in the fur" of a gerbil and to write from a rodent's point of view?

- *Bloom's Taxonomy Level 3 (application) and Level 4 (analysis)*

- *Information Literacy Standard 3 (using information effectively and creatively)*

## Imagine That!

Imagine that each night Melvil and Dewey leave their cage in the library and venture into the school. Where do you think they go, and what happens? What might the gerbils do in *your* classroom at night? In the library? In the principal's office? Write about the secret activities and antics that occur when no humans are watching.

- *Bloom's Taxonomy Level 5 (synthesis)*

- *Information Literacy Standard 3 (using information accurately and creatively)*

# And Then What?

Write or draw the main events that occurred in a Melvil and Dewey story. Now put these incidents in order, as they happened in the story. For fun, you could make a Melvil and Dewey storyboard or comic strip for your class to enjoy.

- *Bloom's Taxonomy Level 1 (knowledge) and Level 3 (application)*

- *Information Literacy Standard 3 (using information accurately and creatively)*

# Danger! Watch Out!

When Mrs. Alden let students take Melvil and Dewey home for the weekend, they faced some dangerous situations. If you were able to take them to your house, how would you care for them and keep them safe? What dangers to gerbils are in your home? Write about a scary situation at your house that Melvil and Dewey must survive.

- *Bloom's Taxonomy Level 6 (evaluation)*

- *Information Literacy Standard 8 (practicing ethical behavior)*

## Feet Tappin', Finger Snappin'
## Gerbil Rhythm

Write a song, rap, or poem about the adventures of Melvil and Dewey.

- *Bloom's Taxonomy Level 5 (synthesis)*

- *Information Literacy Standard 3 (using information accurately and creatively)*

## You're in Charge

Choose one of the Melvil and Dewey stories and write your own original ending. Does your new ending lead to a possible new story?

- *Bloom's Taxonomy Level 5 (synthesis)*

- *Information Literacy Standard 3 (using information accurately and creatively)*

## Where to Next?

Suppose Melvil and Dewey go to a space center, and Melvil pushes a button that he *thinks* says "lunch" but actually says, "launch"? 5... 4... 3... 2... 1 Uh-oh!

Write your own Melvil and Dewey chapters or sequels. Where do the gerbils go on their next adventure?

- *Bloom's Taxonomy Level 5 (synthesis)*

- *Information Literacy Standard 3 (using information accurately and creatively)*

# LET YOUR ARTISTIC SIDE SHINE!
## (GRAB THOSE ART SUPPLIES)

### Move over Mickey and Donald

Draw a comic strip about Melvil and Dewey, with dialogue and captions.

• *Bloom's Taxonomy Level 3 (application) and Level 5 (synthesis)*

• *Information Literacy Standard 3 (using information accurately and creatively)*

## Gerbil's-Eye View

Imagine that the gerbils' cage is on the library checkout desk in your school. Draw this setting first as you see it, and then as it would look to Melvil and Dewey. Talk about point of view and perspective—your own human perspective and gerbil perspective.

- *Bloom's Taxonomy Level 3 (application) and Level 4 (analysis)*

- *Information Literacy Standard 3 (using information accurately and creatively)*

## Melvil and Dewey Do Drama!

Use the sample Melvil and Dewey masks on the following pages, or make your own, and role-play scenes from the stories. You could start with scenes in *Melvil and Dewey in the Chips* where the gerbils don't agree on whether they should leave their cage and explore the school.

Once you're comfortable playing scenes from the books, try writing your own readers' theater scripts!

- *Bloom's Taxonomy Level 3 (application) and Level 5 (synthesis)*

- *Information Literacy Standard 3 (using information accurately and creatively)*

# Bring on the Color!

The drawings in the Melvil and Dewey stories are done in black and white. Here's your chance to have some fun adding whatever colors you wish.

- *Bloom's Taxonomy Level 3 (application) and Level 5 (synthesis)*

- *Information Literacy Standard 3 (using information accurately and creatively)*

# Take a Close Look

Two different artists illustrated the Melvil and Dewey books. Compare and contrast the styles of these two artists.

Both artists used pencil to draw the gerbils. How different might the gerbils have looked if watercolors, poster paint, pen and ink, or pastels were used? Experiment and find out. Which technique do you like best?

- *Bloom's Taxonomy Level 3 (application), Level 4 (analysis), and Level 6 (evaluation)*

- *Information Literacy Standard 3 (using information accurately and creatively)*


## Oh, Those Handsome Fellows!

Paint portraits or sculpt figures of Melvil and Dewey.

- *Bloom's Taxonomy Level 3 (application) and Level 5 (synthesis)*

- *Information Literacy Standard 3 (using information accurately and creatively)*


## Bookmarks!

Decorate and color the bookmarks on the next page, or design your own.

- *Bloom's Taxonomy Level 3 (application) and Level 5 (synthesis)*

- *Information Literacy Standard 3 (using information accurately and creatively)*

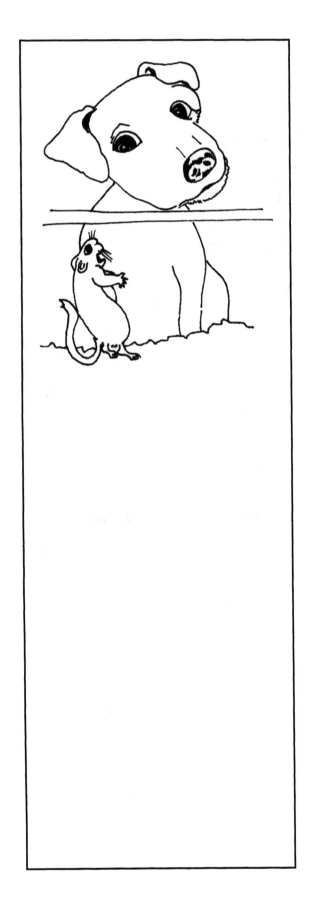

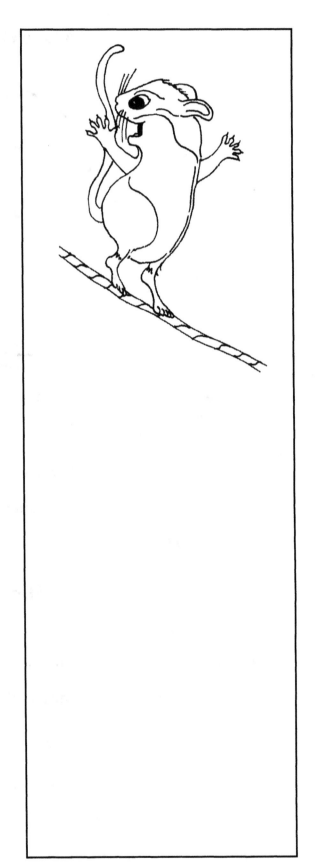

# HANDS ON
# (MAKE IT YOURSELF)

## All Aboard!

Looking around your house and classroom, find materials that you could use to build a small boat or land vehicle, suitable for Melvil and Dewey to use. Construct and demonstrate your vehicle. Does your vehicle give you any ideas for another gerbil adventure?

- *Bloom's Taxonomy Level 5 (synthesis)*

- *Information Literacy Standard 3 (using information accurately and creatively)*

## Dewey Is Caught by a Weasel—
## Move Back Two Spaces!

Create a Melvil and Dewey adventure board game.

- *Bloom's Taxonomy Level 3 (application) and Level 5 (synthesis)*

- *Information Literacy Standard 3 (using information accurately and creatively)*

## Cage Sweet Cage

Design a new cage for Melvil and Dewey. What features do you think each gerbil would want in this new habitat?

- *Bloom's Taxonomy Level 5 (synthesis)*

- *Information Literacy Standard 3 (using information accurately and creatively)*

## Puppets

Use the sample puppets on the next page, or make your own—using socks, paper maché, styrofoam, brown paper bags, or whatever you would like to use (how about potatoes!) and then and write your own puppet show scripts of Melvil and Dewey adventures.

• *Bloom's Taxonomy Level 3 (application) and Level 5 (synthesis)*

• *Information Literacy Standard 3 (using information accurately and creatively)*

## Gerbil Jumbles and Puzzles

Have fun with the word puzzles that follow, and then create your own word jumbles, word searches, or crossword puzzles using names, places, and events from the stories.

• *Bloom's Taxonomy Level 5 (synthesis)*

• *Information Literacy Standard 3 (using information accurately and creatively)*

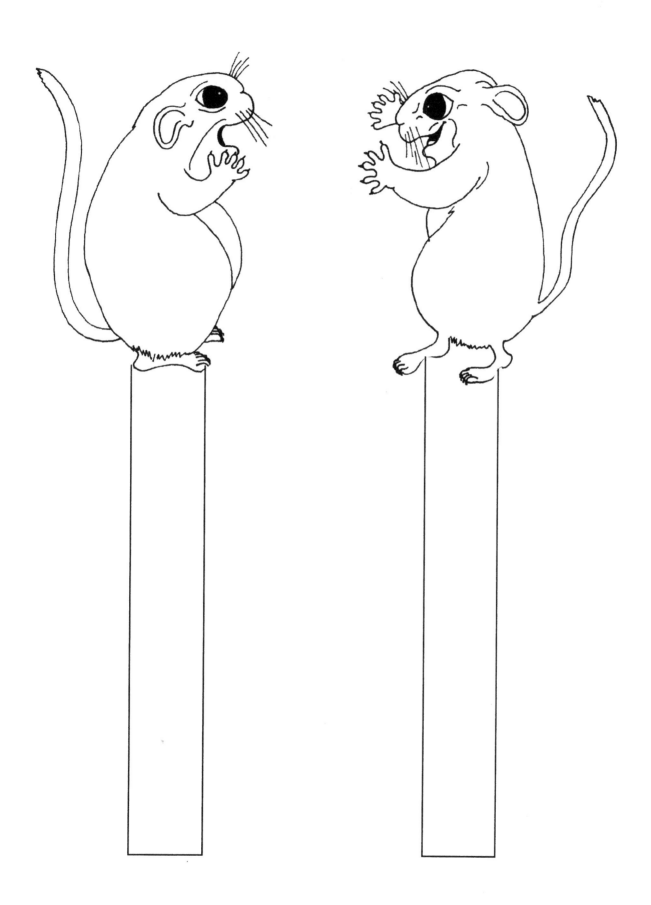

# MELVIL AND DEWEY WORD SEARCH

## (Across and Down)

```
E  O  L  E  W  A  L  A  Y  E  N  R  E  E  F
C  P  S  E  D  M  G  L  E  E  M  W  A  A  A
L  E  S  L  E  N  N  S  L  F  E  I  E  B  B
B  T  W  J  W  B  S  P  I  I  L  J  A  K  E
B  E  A  V  E  R  L  M  B  S  V  R  W  A  W
K  A  L  L  Y  W  O  N  R  H  I  E  I  R  B
E  A  L  N  A  B  I  G  A  I  L  Y  S  L  I
T  C  O  M  P  U  T  E  R  N  I  E  A  W  I
L  I  W  A  A  A  A  R  Y  G  E  R  A  V  E
D  K  H  S  Y  M  N  B  W  E  S  P  B  B  T
S  S  A  H  M  I  K  I  B  A  E  L  F  A  E
R  O  W  E  A  S  E  L  I  L  R  I  H  L  G
I  K  K  R  I  L  I  W  L  I  R  A  L  M  N
A  L  D  E  N  D  K  D  E  L  E  M  V  G  N
S  N  A  K  E  I  S  U  A  G  F  E  O  I  I
```

☐ MELVIL        ☐ DEWEY         ☐ LIBRARY
☐ TANK          ☐ PETE          ☐ ABIGAIL
☐ MASHER        ☐ FISHING       ☐ MAINE
☐ GERBIL        ☐ HAWK          ☐ WEASEL
☐ SWALLOW       ☐ BEAVER        ☐ COMPUTER
☐ JAKE          ☐ ALDEN         ☐ SNAKE

# MELVIL AND DEWEY WORD SEARCH

(Includes backward and diagonal words)

```
P  E  S  B  L  C  E  I  Y  E  S  A  S  E  R
E  W  T  G  B  I  S  E  I  S  N  A  K  E  I
P  B  K  L  N  M  E  E  W  J  A  R  H  S  E
S  F  W  B  E  A  A  N  E  E  H  S  V  L  K
G  E  R  L  N  E  N  I  E  T  A  H  E  S  A
I  L  V  F  G  Y  S  J  N  M  I  W  K  L  H
K  A  N  K  I  E  L  B  A  E  O  P  E  C  R
E  R  S  A  W  W  R  O  B  L  W  G  E  O  E
I  W  A  L  D  E  N  B  L  V  N  D  A  M  L
K  N  P  A  V  D  K  A  I  I  A  C  B  P  L
U  L  A  A  G  K  W  A  H  L  B  W  I  U  W
B  N  E  A  N  S  A  S  J  R  L  R  G  T  R
K  B  T  E  W  E  I  E  E  L  E  S  A  E  W
M  E  E  A  W  F  R  L  N  L  G  N  I  R  T
S  E  P  I  M  H  I  L  L  V  K  H  L  E  Y
```

|  |  |  |
|---|---|---|
| ☐ MELVIL | ☐ DEWEY | ☐ LIBRARY |
| ☐ TANK | ☐ PETE | ☐ ABIGAIL |
| ☐ MASHER | ☐ FISHING | ☐ MAINE |
| ☐ GERBIL | ☐ HAWK | ☐ WEASEL |
| ☐ SWALLOW | ☐ BEAVER | ☐ COMPUTER |
| ☐ JAKE | ☐ ALDEN | ☐ SNAKE |

### *GERBIL JUMBLE!*

1. PECMURTO _____

2. EMLILV _____

3. HNGFISI _____

4. EWYED _____

5. BIARYLR _____

6. BILIGAA _____

7. HRESAM _____

8. KTNA _____

9. EGILRB _____

10. EPTE _____

# aMAZing!

Rodents are sometimes given the challenge of finding their way through a maze to locate a treat at the end. If you have available pet rodents, construct a maze and see how they do. If no rodents are handy, draw a maze and ask your friends to try it out. You could even make a life-size maze out of cardboard or other materials for your friends to enjoy.

- *Bloom's Taxonomy Level 5 (synthesis)*

- *Information Literacy Standard 3 (using information accurately and creatively)*

# Mix It Up! Gerbil Food for Kids

Kids and adventuresome gerbils have lots in common, including a taste for crunchy snacks. Make yourself some!

- 2 cups of nuts—your favorite kinds (cashews, almonds, walnuts, pecans are all tasty choices. No peanuts, please.)

- ½ cup of seeds, both sunflower and shelled pumpkin seeds

- 1 cup of raisins, golden or dark (or combine both)

- ½ cup of dried cranberries

- ½ cup of chopped dates

Get a big bowl and mix everything together. Dig in!

This is how Melvil likes it, but you can change proportions and add other ingredients.

- *Bloom's Taxonomy Level 3 (application) and Level 5 (synthesis)*

- *Information Literacy Standard 3 (using information accurately and creatively)*

# LET'S TALK
## (SHARING THOUGHTS AND ANALYSES)

### Literature Circles, Book Discussions, Guided Reading

Book discussions are fun and help readers to get more from a story. The Melvil and Dewey stories are examples of fantasy. What makes a story fantasy? Can you think of other examples of this genre?

Discuss decision making—Melvil and Dewey have to think quickly to save themselves in dangerous situations. How do you think you might have acted in those situations? Would you have made different choices?

Explore options for continuing the Melvil and Dewey series. What new story ideas might be developed into sequels?

- *Bloom's Taxonomy Level 1 (knowledge), Level 2 (comprehension), and Level 4 (analysis)*

- *Information Literacy Standard 2 (evaluating information) and Standard 5 (appreciating literature)*

# Melvil, How Did You Feel?

How about trying your hand at interviewing our favorite gerbils? Try this: have your librarian or teacher demonstrate how an interviewer might conduct an interview with Melvil and Dewey. Have two students play the gerbils' parts and be interviewed to learn more about their wants and wishes, fears, and (yes) phobias. After the demonstration interview, divide into groups of three and do your own interviews. Then come together as a group and talk about what the interviewers learned about the two very different gerbil brothers.

- *Bloom's Taxonomy Level 3 (application) and Level 5 (synthesis)*

- *Information Literacy Standard 3 (using information accurately and creatively)*

## What Would *You* Do?

We each have very different personalities, traits, and habits. Melvil and Dewey certainly do. Which gerbil do you think you are more like, and in what ways? Give examples.

Put yourself in one of the gerbil adventures. How would you handle their predicaments?

- *Bloom's Taxonomy Level 3 (application) and Level 4 (analysis)*

- *Information Literacy Standard 3 (using information effectively and creatively)*

## Survivor!

In *Melvil and Dewey Gone Fishin'*, the gerbils are stranded on an island. What other ways might they have gotten off the island to save themselves? If you were stranded on an island, what would *you* do?

- *Bloom's Taxonomy Level 5 (synthesis)*

- *Information Literacy Standard 3 (using information accurately and creatively)*

# Watching Melvil's Weight

More than half of the people (and a few gerbils) are overweight in the United States. Think of some ways that you could help Melvil lose weight. Get together in groups to discuss your ideas and then report back to the class.

- *Bloom's Taxonomy Level 3 (application)*

- *Information Literacy Standard 3 (using information accurately and creatively)*

# ABOUT THE AUTHOR AND ILLUSTRATOR
## (WHO'S WHO BEHIND THE SCENES)

## Author Pamela Curtis Swallow

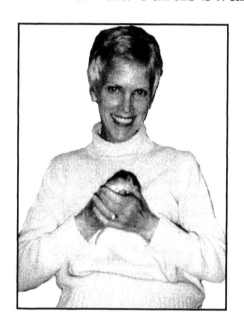

I've always liked rodents. I don't scream when I see a mouse. When I was younger, I had pet hamsters, gerbils, and an orphaned red squirrel. Later, during the years when I worked as a school librarian, I had gerbils in my library. If you're guessing that the character of Mrs. Alden is based on me, you're right. But there are two other characters whose personalities are also part of me. It's those rodents! I'm a lot like both Melvil and Dewey. I love adventure and excitement, like Dewey, but I also like to sit down with a snack while I think things over, just as Melvil does.

Growing up in Connecticut, I was a tomboy. I rode horses, played sports with the neighborhood boys, and dreamed of becoming a ranch hand. No one who knew me then ever imagined that I'd end up having two professions where it's good to be able to sit still and keep quiet. Well, to be truthful, I *still* have trouble with those two things! But when something is important to me, I keep at it. While I'm working on a book, I get up a lot and walk my dogs and water my plants . . . but I always come back to my stories and persist until I'm finished.

When I look out the window of the writing office in my New Jersey home to the farm across the lane, I can watch yaks, llamas, emus, miniature horses and donkeys, pigmy goats, ducks, peacocks, a pot-bellied pig, and even a bandicoot. In the fields and woods next to my house, I can see deer, foxes, raccoons, opossums, hawks, wild turkeys, pheasants, and even coyotes. My yard is home to rabbits, squirrels, mice, moles, and very fat groundhogs. It's no wonder there are always animals in my books.

I live with my husband, Bill; my two dogs, Bailey and Maggie; my two cats Katie and Emily; and my two computers, Thor and Odin. It is my hope that I will be writing books for many years to come.

## More about the Author

What else can you learn about the author of the Melvil and Dewey stories? What other books has she written?

Check her Web site (www.PamelaCurtisSwallow. com) for behind-the-scenes information.

- *Bloom's Taxonomy Level 1 (knowledge)*

- Information Literacy Standard 1 (accessing information)

## Illustrator Lorena Eliasen

Drawing gerbils was challenging yet fun for me. *Melvil and Dewey Gone Fishin'* is the second book I have illustrated since graduating from Parsons School of Design in 2002. The first was a pop-up book that I also wrote, *The Chameleon and the Dragonfly*.

This book was a big challenge for me because my husband, David, and I just had our very first baby four months ago. Luckily, baby Salomé likes to sleep through the night, so I can work while she rests. Working at night is not so bad. Lots of famous people work at night. Do you know that the Spanish artist Goya worked mostly at night?

As a little girl, I did not draw very well. I still remember the awful little princesses I used to draw and how frustrated I felt when I didn't get them right. I know now, though, that practice makes perfect. It is easy to practice when you really love what you are doing.

I was born in Ecuador but have lived in New York for seven years. It was hard to leave everything back home and learn a new language. But now I absolutely love New York—it's my adopted home.

I can't complain about my life. I have a wonderful daughter, a great husband, a beloved family, and the opportunity to do something I really love—*Draw!*

## More about the Illustrator

Can you find out more about the new illustrator of the Melvil and Dewey stories? See what you can learn by visiting her Web site www.lorenaeliasen.com.

• *Bloom's Taxonomy Level 1 (knowledge)*

• *Information Literacy Standard 1 (accessing information)*

# ADVICE ON GERBILS AS PETS
# (STUDENT-TO-STUDENT SUGGESTIONS)

For several years, Ryan Smith, age twelve, was a library student of Pam Swallow's. The two of them share an enthusiasm for animals, and in particular for gerbils, which Ryan now raises. He says that he decided to breed gerbils for two reasons: because he likes them and because he thought that they could be a way to make money. Ryan has learned about more than just gerbils during this experience. He has also learned about responsibility—he must buy food, bedding, and equipment; he has to make sure his gerbils have a proper diet and fresh water; he makes certain that they stay healthy; he must clean their cages; and finally, he has to be careful to control his gerbil population.

Ryan lives in Hunterdon County, New Jersey, with his parents, his two brothers, his dog, and his gerbils. He likes sports—in particular, soccer, basketball, lacrosse, and snowboarding.

## Ryan's Tips on Gerbil Care

1. If you want to have a gerbil for a pet, think about getting two. Gerbils are colony animals, and they like company. They are ready for adoption at about six to eight weeks old. It's best if the gerbils already know each other and get along. Have a breeder or a veterinarian check the gender of the gerbils, so you'll know what to expect!

2. A ten-gallon tank is a good size for two gerbils. Be sure that the tank has a wire mesh lid because gerbils can jump! Remember a water bottle. All animals need to drink.

3. Do not use cedar or pine shavings in the cage. Use corncob, aspen, or a product called Carefresh. Gerbils also like to shred plain white unscented tissue for their nests.

4. Gerbils get bored if they have nothing to do. Put an exercise wheel, chew sticks, cans, and cardboard tubes in their cage.

5. Gerbils are sensitive to cold. Watch the temperature and keep them away from drafts.

6. Feed gerbils a good premixed blend. For treats, you can hand-feed sunflower seeds and Cheerios. Don't overdo the fruits and veggies, or you'll be cleaning the cage a lot!

7. Handle your gerbils gently. Begin slowly by putting your hand low, on their level, and letting them climb onto it. Do not move quickly or swoop down from above, because that can scare them. You will gradually be able to take them from their cage—but stay seated so that you do not drop them.

8. Don't bathe your gerbils in water. They will groom themselves. But if they look as if they need more than that, pour a bit of chinchilla dust mixed with clean sand into a small flat pan. They will do the rest.

9. Do not introduce a new gerbil to an established group or pair. They will probably not get along.

10. A gerbil mother gets scared if you disturb the babies too much. She might even hurt them if she is made to feel too nervous.

11. Separate gerbil babies from their parents at about five weeks. Also separate males and females at that time.

12. If your gerbils have babies and you cannot keep all of them, make sure that you give or sell them only to people who will take good care of them.

# The End?

There's no need for this to be the end. You can go back through the different activities and try new ones. Or do some of them again—practice makes perfect. How about thinking up your own original activities. You could try them out and then trade activities with your friends. You could make up activity packets for other books that you like. This is just the beginning!

Printed in the USA
CPSIA information can be obtained
at www.ICGtesting.com
LVHW080839171024
794056LV00006B/1428